OWL at SCHOO

for Rebecca

OWL at SCHOOL

by Helen Nicoll
and Jan Pieńkowski

PUFFIN BOOKS

SWOOP
CRUNCH
Ooops!

He'll have to go to school
Crashed again!

Come on! You'll love it

Here is your dinner
Wrap up warm
Hurry! We'll be late

Bye! Be good
Are you new?
Meg took Owl to school

Hello Snowy

There were 4 other owls in the class

The teacher was called Mr Winko

The first lesson was swooping and pouncing

Now don't all pounce at once

ATTACK!

The bell rang for dinner

They all had different food

Mole
in the hole

Shrew
stew

Yuk!
Have some of mine
No fear
Rat pasty
Stuffed toad
Welsh rabbit

Ms Bats taught night flying

Bank between the branches

Owl
was
top
in
soaring

middling
at
hovering

good
at
diving

and
bottom
in
swimming

It was Sports Night

Owl was anxious

At home
Meg was making
a special hat

Meg
brought
Mog
to watch
the
School Sports

Charming charming
Good luck Owl

Everybody noticed Meg's hat

Owl won the night flight race

He asked
all his
friends
to tea

Can I come again tomorrow ?
I won
Show off

After tea they all went home

Goodbye Snowy

Goodbye!